South Arbor Charter Academy
Media Center
Ypsilanti, MI 48197

Motorcycles

Andrea Rivera

abdopublishing.com

Published by Abdo Zoom™, PO Box 398166, Minneapolis, Minnesota 55439. Copyright © 2017 by Abdo Consulting Group, Inc. International copyrights reserved in all countries. No part of this book may be reproduced in any form without written permission from the publisher. Abdo Zoom™ is a trademark and logo of Abdo Consulting Group, Inc.

Printed in the United States of America, North Mankato, Minnesota
102016
012017

Cover Photo: Shutterstock Images
Interior Photos: Shutterstock Images, 1, 12, 18, 19; Pavel Lysenko/Shutterstock Images, 4; iStockphoto, 5, 7, 21; Don Wilkie/iStockphoto, 6; Action Sports Photography/Shutterstock Images, 8; Phillip Rubino/Shutterstock Images, 9, 10–11; Anna Omelchenko/iStockphoto, 13; Pas Photography/Shutterstock Images, 14; James Steidl/Shutterstock Images, 15; Don Pablo/Shutterstock Images, 17

Editor: Brienna Rossiter
Series Designer: Madeline Berger
Art Direction: Dorothy Toth

Publisher's Cataloging-in-Publication Data
Names: Rivera, Andrea, author.
Title: Motorcycles / by Andrea Rivera.
Description: Minneapolis, MN : Abdo Zoom, 2017. | Series: Powerful machines | Includes bibliographical references and index.
Identifiers: LCCN 2016949154 | ISBN 9781680799484 (lib. bdg.) |
    ISBN 9781624025341 (ebook) | ISBN 9781624025907 (Read-to-me ebook)
Subjects: LCSH: Motorcycles--Juvenile literature.
Classification: DDC 629.227/5--dc23
LC record available at http://lccn.loc.gov/2016949154

Table of Contents

Science 4

Technology. 8

Engineering 12

Art 14

Math 16

Key Stats. 20

Glossary 22

Booklinks 23

Index 24

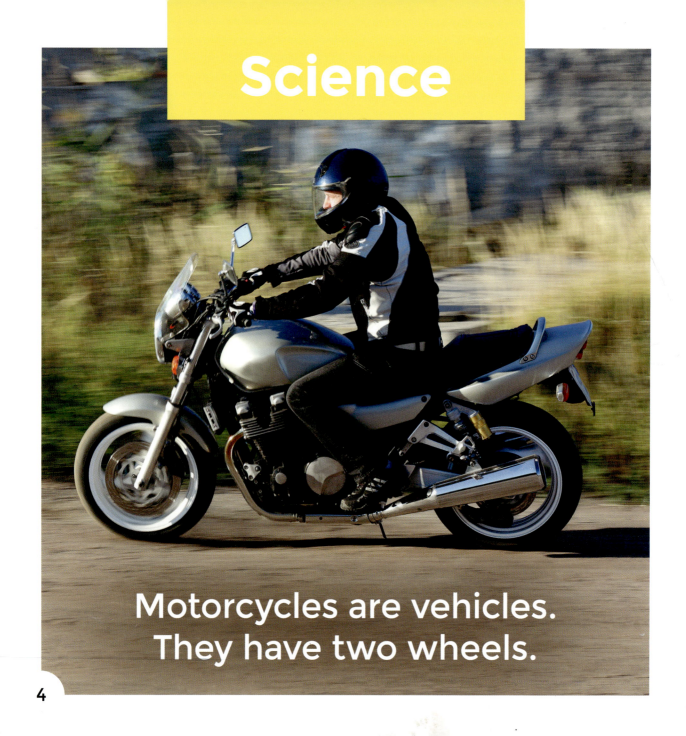

Science

Motorcycles are vehicles.
They have two wheels.

The front wheel steers the bike.

The back wheel is usually bigger.

It gets power from the **engine**.

Technology

Pro stock motorcycles are built for racing.

Their special shape makes them more **aerodynamic**.

Their engines are strong. Computers make sure they are working well.

Engineering

A motorcycle's **fork** is made of metal tubes.

The tubes slide in and out. They help the rider not feel bumps in the road.

Art

Some people make **choppers**. Many choppers have long forks.

They often have high handlebars.
But no two are alike.

Math

Cubic centimeters are used to measure the space inside an engine. Stronger engines have more space.

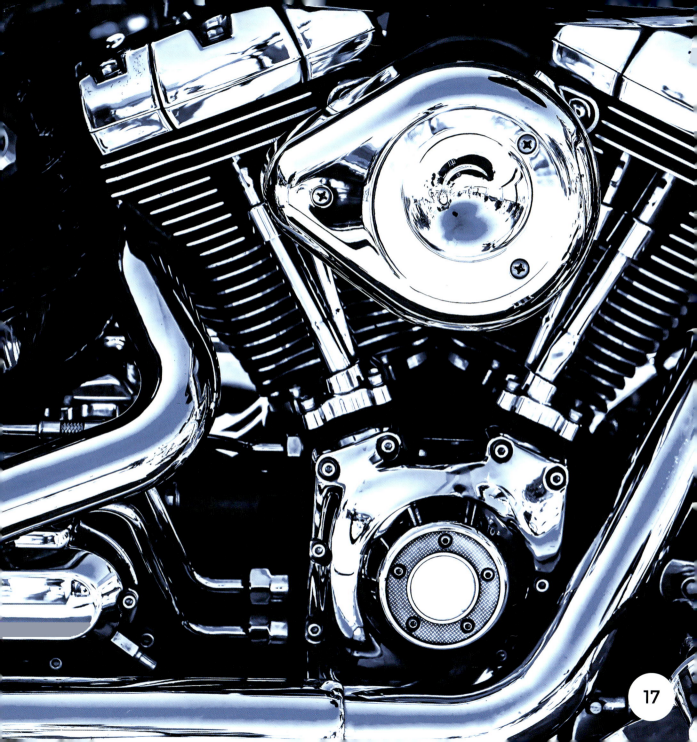

A dirt bike's engine can have around 600 cubic centimeters.

Sport bikes have bigger engines. Some have more than 1,000 cubic centimeters.

- The first motorcycle available to the public was built in 1894.

- Dirt bikes weigh less than other motorcycles. Most are less than 300 pounds (136 kg).

- Sport bikes can go very fast. They are lightweight, but they have very strong engines.

- Some pro stock motorcycles can go from zero to 100 miles per hour (161 kmh) in two seconds!

Glossary

aerodynamic - having a shape that helps something move through the air.

chopper - a specially built motorcycle that often has a long fork.

engine - a machine that uses energy to run or move something.

fork - the part of a motorcycle that connects the front wheel to the motorcycle's body.

Booklinks

For more information on **motorcycles**, please visit booklinks.abdopublishing.com

Learn even more with the Abdo Zoom STEAM database. Check out **abdozoom.com** for more information.

Index

choppers, 14

cubic centimeters, 16, 18, 19

dirt bike, 18

engine, 7, 10, 16, 18, 19

fork, 12, 14

handlebars, 15

pro stock, 8

racing, 8

sport bikes, 19

wheels, 4, 5, 6